HOW (NOT) TO LIVE IN SUBURBIA

Annie Siddons

HOW (NOT) TO LIVE IN SUBURBIA

OBERON BOOKS
LONDON

WWW.OBERONBOOKS.COM

First published in 2017 by Oberon Books Ltd
521 Caledonian Road, London N7 9RH
Tel: +44 (0) 20 7607 3637 / Fax: +44 (0) 20 7607 3629
e-mail: info@oberonbooks.com
www.oberonbooks.com

A catalogue record for this book is available from the British
Library.

PB ISBN: 9781786822529
E ISBN: 9781786822536

Cover design by Claire Nolan

Foreword

In summer 2014, I became dangerously lonely. It was not only humiliating but surprising for me. I'm gregarious. I have good social skills. I love hard and well. So I swallowed my pride and tried to talk about my loneliness to my friends.

It was clear from my unofficial study that talking about loneliness felt treacherous. There was a received understanding at the time that old people were lonely. The elderly are, of course, disproportionately lonely. I'm not in any sense knocking elder loneliness. But it felt that our acceptance of and compassion for elder loneliness was a way of distancing ourselves from our own.

It seemed important that if I was going to make a show about loneliness, that it should be honest and autobiographical and also funny – that because the stigma attached to being lonely was so great I needed to exorcise it by being really frank about my own downward spiral. I'd never done an autobiographical show before, but the content demanded it.

My own loneliness, I knew, stemmed in part from being exiled in a life that didn't feel like my own – the suburbia I'm talking about is a metaphorical space but is also a geographical reality – and so the show is in part a love letter to my much maligned and much adored city. Writing this foreword today after the recent terror attacks and the atrocity of the Grenfell Tower Fire, that heterogeneity and tolerance that, to me, is the spirit of London, is being shaken to its very foundations by other, egregious agendas – for instance of social cleansing, of fear of other, of contempt for the poor. But Londoners are tough, resilient, angry, and love their city, and they will not stop fighting to ensure London keeps her integrity.

When I was in Edinburgh 2014 doing my previous show, *Raymondo*, I had met Richard DeDomenici, whose neeky pyschogeographical love and knowledge of cities, playfulness, satirical bent, keen eye, and filmic prowess, meant he became the obvious person for me to collaborate with on this show. Richard directed all the films that are in this show, and because video is such an important part of it we've put some stills in to give you a flavour.

Since we first made the show, in the way of things, the conversation about loneliness in the media has broadened. It's now known, for instance, that chronic loneliness has serious physical as well as mental health implications – that many different demographics are susceptible to it – that it can be self perpetuating – that it can be life threatening – cf the much quoted "15 cigarettes" soundbite – that it often has no relationship to existing social skills. There have been some brilliant books written about it – here I'd like to shout out two: John Cacioppo, the Chicago based neuroscientist, writes limpidly about loneliness as a biosociological phenomenon. I read his book – aptly titled *Loneliness* – late into making the show and was surprised and oddly relieved at how he seemed to be describing me.

The second is Olivia Laing's *The Lonely City* which is a much more subjective, poetic take on the author's own loneliness and contains some absolutely perfect sentences: "Loneliness is personal, and it is also political. Loneliness is collective: it is a city…. What matters is kindness…what matters is solidarity."

All theatre is of course collaborative, but making this show, in which I air my most befouled laundry and try and make good, accessible art from it, has been more collaborative than most. I'd like to thank everyone who supported the show from its inception to its full realisation – Brian and the Camden People's Theatre Family, Emma and the Ferment Family, Pulse Festival, China Plate, Latitude Festival, Ruby, Sarah and everyone at Derby Theatre, Arts Council England, New Wolsey Theatre, Peggy Ramsay Foundation, Colchester Arts Centre, Summerhall, Krissi Musiol, Pamela Qualter, Soho Theatre. And individually I'd like to thank the excellent human beings who work with me and who helped me shape this show and also helped me survive the making of it. These are – Richard DeDomenici, Anthony Roberts, Adam Robertson, Andy Purves, my producer Jen Smethurst, Justin Audibert my regular director, and most of all Nicki Hobday, who joined us to play "all other women" in the videos and ended up co-directing the show, playing me in the stage version of the show, overseeing our marketing campaign, and becoming my sometime nanny, housemate, Walrus dispeller and closest friend: I owe a debt of gratitude to all these people, and to Nic especially.

I'd like to dedicate this book to the lonely and those who help them, particularly all Samaritans, particularly the Samaritans of Kingston branch.

Annie Siddons, June 2017

How (Not) to Live in Suburbia was first performed as a scratch in June 2015 At Pulse Festival. Subsequent scratches were performed at Camden People's Theatre and Bristol Ferment. The show was commissioned by New Wolsey and supported by Bristol Ferment, Camden People's Theatre, Arts Council England and Peggy Ramsay Foundation. It previewed at festivals during summer 2016, including Latitude, then opened at Summerhall, Edinburgh Fringe, 2016. In November 2016 it formed the basis of a Symposium on Loneliness held at UCLAN, Preston. It played at Soho Theatre in February 2017 and returns there to start the UK tour in summer 2017.

How (Not) to Live in Suburbia opened on August 6th 2016 at Summerhall as part of Edinburgh Fringe 2016.

Written by Annie Siddons
Performed by Annie Siddons and Adam Robertson
Directed by Justin Audibert and Nicki Hobday
Produced by Jen Smethurst
Films directed by Richard DeDomenici

Featuring Jack Darell (Jay), Nicki Hobday (Claire, Elle, Woman with Dog, Shona, Woman with Cupcakes, Seal), Anthony Roberts (Graeme, Border Guard), Adam Robertson (Walrus), and Bette the dog.

Production Assistant	Sophie Bramley
Post production Assistant	Ellie Stamp
Lighting designer	Andy Purves
Technician	Jen Smethurst

How (Not) to Live in Suburbia was first performed by Annie Siddons and Nicki Hobday in London at the Soho Theatre on 13 February 2017. All subsequent performances have been by Annie Siddons and Nicki Hobday.

In this show, the live performance is divided between two performers. Annie, the writer, and subject of the show, who narrates, and Nicki, who plays the character of Annie.

All text that appears in **bold** indicates the content of the video being projected on stage. Everything else is being performed live on stage, unless stated otherwise.

A woman, ANNIE, is drinking in a pub. She looks unhappy. She's flanked by a SEAL and a WALRUS. The film plays in slow motion. Justin Bieber's 'One Less Lonely Girl' plays.

Annie: One evening, a few years ago, I had a visitor…

WALRUS enters film.

Interior, ANNIE's house. A messy, lived in house with evidence of kids everywhere. ANNIE is reading books of self improvement and smoking. There's a knock at the door. She goes to open it. Standing at her doorway is a massive WALRUS.

ANNIE: **Who the fuck are you?**

WALRUS: **I'm the Walrus of Loneliness.**

ANNIE: **What?**

WALRUS: **I'm the Walrus of Loneliness. Let me in.**

He pushes past her.

ANNIE: Some years before that I'd moved with my family to a leafy southwestern suburb of London. We'd moved for my husband's job. And a couple of years after that, in the middle of a shitstorm of life events, our marriage uttered its death rattle.

I fucking LOVE London.

FILM: LONDON

Film montage showing a day in London, from the early dawn hawking of Smithfield Meat Market, to the city, to the Greenwich peninsula, to Pellici in Bethnal Green to a young muslim woman having coffee in Covent Garden, to

a secret beach on the Thames. Buildings, art, hustle, people, heterogeneity. People of different ethnicities, social classes, ages. The prostitutes' cemetery, some city gents having their shoes shined, young waiters, Soho. A whistle stop one minute homage to London, ending in a gay pub in Soho watching London's oldest Elvis impersonator. Dave Elvis.

She contains multitudes. She is squalid, stenchy and ancient. She is modern, violent, anonymous, neighbourly, she is Babel. She is hustle, art, optimism, and hubris. She is change and development, she is sass and subcultures and an ever-evolving vernacular. She is law and disorder, she is convention and anarchy, and she is HISTORY. She is the blowsy, plump, secret-holding river. She is the tolerance of freaks and outsiders. She is a claret drinking velvet clad red faced gent and a baby rudeboy trying to make sense. She is your sartorially daring BFF. London is an overripe brothel madam with a Postdoctorate. She is the best conversation, the wittiest companion. She will delight and surprise you – and steal your wallet. She will make you try harder, keep you on your toes, beat you up and love you like no other. She is an old soul with nine million beating hearts from all the corners of the globe, whom she has enticed with her dirty promises. She has been the one constant thing in my life, my great love: my London.

And now I was living *allegedly* in London, yet so not in her – too far west to be on my huge map –

VISUALS: A MAP SHOWING THE WHOLE OF LONDON WITH TWICKENHAM: HOME OF RUGBY BEYOND THE EDGE OF THE MAP.

the outer, genteel, ruffled petticoats of my brothely love – zone 5, mofos! Twickenham: Home of Rugby.

FILM 3 SUBURBIA
Film montage showing the monoculture of suburbia: the dominance of the rugby culture, whiteness, massive houses, Ocado deliveries, Estate agents, boojie gift shops, expensive

gyms, even more expensive beauty treatments, the stadium
towering over everything.

My daughters had moved five times already in their short
lives – and they had then been caught in the slipstream of
the shitstorm. So I decided to stay in Twickenham: Home
of Rugby – or THOR, as I like to call it – in order to allow
the girls to build on the roots they had begun to lay down
for the very first time. It felt like the right thing to do. It felt
mature.

The wish to protect my daughters' anonymity has meant
we are representing them here by miniature olive trees – a
nod to their Mediterranean heritage and lustrous foliage.

FILM 4
Olive Trees outside ANNIE's house.

There they are. My beautiful, brilliant, hilarious daughters.
The arboriculturally nerdy amongst you will know, of
course, that olive trees have very SHALLOW root systems.
This means they can suck up nourishment from hostile
environments – but are also prone to exposure.

The shitstorm had totally laid waste to my work capacity.
Absolutely Cock All was happening professionally, and my
agent, Verity, who smoked long, thin cigarettes, and was
pretty much permanently on a skiing holiday, sent me this
email.

VISUALS: VERITY SKIING.

V/O:

Annie

Theatre is a Darwinian profession. It's survival of
the fittest. I know you have been having some little
personal problems but you're going to have to pull
your finger out and write something quickly that I
can sell. I'm not interested in having one hit wonders
on my books. The other day someone said "Annie

who?" and I can't have that so put your head down
and write. I know you can do it. Lickety Spit.

Thanks

Verity.

XO XO X

So I set to work.

FILM 5
*ANNIE tries to write in her shed. Montage of writerly
frustration and procrastination. At the end of the montage,
she picks up a book, called 'HOW TO BE AN ARTIST' by
Michael Atavar, and reads from it.*

ANNIE: *(Reading.)* If it's really not working after five
years, try a new career.

Writing…is a solitary activity.

FILM 6 SUBURBIA MONTAGE 2
*Another snapshot of suburbia. Swarms of kids coming out
of school. The ridiculous beauty of Richmond park. People
running. People rowing. People cycling. Obsession with
fitness and sport. Nuclear families everywhere.*

Meanwhile my daughters were benefitting from their
leafy surroundings. They were enjoying the wide open
spaces, the good schools and nurseries, the bike rides,
the atmosphere of compulsive sportiness, and the safe,
monocultural, nuclear neighbourhood of THOR. And
they were laying down roots. And they were making good
friends.

I had friends too. Gorgeous, delicious friends. They mainly
fell into two categories:

Category One: Not here!

All my childless artist friends seemed to live in NEW
CROSS –

VISUALS: A MAP APPEARS, SHOWING A SHINY
MAGICAL AREA OF LONDON CALLED NEW CROSS.

– which is, as you may know, a magical enclave in
the southeast of London populated only by artists and
unicorns. There are rules about leaving New Cross which
are these – you're not allowed to – unless it is to go to
other equally magical parts of London. So whilst a lot of
this was happening –

VISUALS: TEXTS FROM MY PALS.

Siddz are you coming to D's party?
Siddz, gig on Friday, you in?
Longtime bitch, where you at?

None of which I could avail myself of, because of the Olive
Trees, the distance, and the cost of childcare – so was a lot
of this…

VISUALS: SCREENSHOTS – TEXTS FROM MY PALS
SHOWING THEIR RELUCTANCE TO MAKE IT TO
THOR.

I'm so tired, why you live zone 5?
Trains are fucked, some rugby ting, can't make it
Someone's killed themselves – bleak (sad face emoji)

The second category of friends was this:

NUCLEAR – FUNCTIONALLY GROWN UP

These fellow travellers were people like my University
friend Lily. They were holding on to relationships, hustling
for work during a recession, raising families, and caring
for elderly parents. They had strict work timetables,
grooming regimens, batch cooking rotas, and community
commitments. Their lives were regulated ones of heroic
compromise. We could go months without contact. My
love for them was deep, and theirs was for me too, but in
the day to day, that love could feel somewhat theoretical.

So I decided to do two things. The first was to write a Manifesto.

Enter NICKI, my co-performer, dressed as me.

NICKI-AS-ANNIE:

My Manifesto…My <u>ANNIEFESTO</u>.

1. Be a brilliant mother.

2. Make good art.

(And make a living from it.)

(And be acclaimed by a small, or preferably large, group of people because of it.)

(And be known by the wider public or – at least respected by your peers in the same field.)

(And make a difference with it.)

3. Love and Connect.

ANNIE: – and the Second thing was to throw myself wholeheartedly into life in Twickenham: Home of Rugby, in the hope that I could find my tribe, some echo of my London, some scent of home. So – I attended a Street Party in honour of HRH baby George Windsor.

Oliver Cromwell. ANNIE attends a royalist street party dressed as Oliver Cromwell and is pelted with cupcakes and chased off.

I went to a local toddler group.

Interior. Toddler Group. SHONA, the toddler group leader, is there.

SHONA: *(Singing.)* Weeeeeee've taken our coats off one by one. Right sleeve off with a tug tug tug.

ANNIE enters, with Olive Tree, late.

SHONA: Hallooooo, halloooo.

ANNIE: Hello, sorry I'm late.

SHONA: Weeeeer'e takING our coats off one by one. And I'll hang them up for you. We were just about to sing some songs. Let me give you a wee little name badge.

I'll just pop that on there for you.

ANNIE: Thanks.

SHONA: We've got one for Olive Tree's mummy as well.

ANNIE: It's Annie.

SHONA: I'll just pop that on there for you. *(She presses the name badge a little too hard onto ANNIE's chest.)*

ANNIE: My, my name is Annie.

SHONA: *(Sings.)* Olive Tree's mummy's got a name badge on. Zoom, zoom, zoom, we're going to the moon. 5! 4! 3! *(Indicates to ANNIE to contribute the next number.)*

ANNIE: 2.

SHONA: 2, 1, blaaaaast offffff! We're blasting off to the moon! Come on Olive Tree's mummy, put a wee bit more effort into it! We're blasting off to the moon!

Who's a princess?

Olive Tree's a princess.

Who's a princess?

No Toby, you're a prince.

The Olive Tree palpably doesn't want to be a princess. ANNIE feels very uncomfortable, and gets up to go.

ANNIE: Sorry.

ANNIE and Olive Tree go.

SHONA: *(Singing.)* Don't cry princess. No Toby, you're a prince. Who else is a princess?

Sophie's a princess! And Toby's a prince!

ANNIE: And I tried communing with nature.

ANNIE with deer. ANNIE dressed as a deer, trying to mingle with the deer in Richmond Park. They are aloof and disinterested.

Oh come onnah!

These attempts at fitting in were not an unmitigated success, so next I decided to try a book group. I like books. The woman who ran the book group was Claire. She was married to Graeme. A few weeks after the first book group meeting, in order to cement my commitment to the group, I did something I had never knowingly done before. I went to a dinner party.

DINNER PARTY
ANNIE's just coming out of the bathroom. An older man, GRAEME, is there.

GRAEME: **Annie, Annie, Annie!**

ANNIE: **Hello Graeme.**

GRAEME: **Mmmm. Now what starsign are you?**

ANNIE: **What starsign am I? I'm a Cancer, but I don't really believe in starsigns.**

GRAEME: **That makes sense.**

ANNIE: **Why is that then?**

GRAEME: **Because I can tell you've got an absolutely enormous rack.**

ANNIE: **What?**

GRAEME: **Now, what about a little kiss for Graeme? Hmmm? What about a little kiss for Graeme?**

ANNIE: **No. No little kiss for Graeme.**

GRAEME: **What about a little kiss for Graeme?**

ANNIE: No little kiss for Graeme. No little kiss for Graeme. *(Rebuffs him.)*

GRAEME: But you work in theatre, you basically put out for a living.

ANNIE: What?! I'm going to get Claire to call you a cab, alright Graeme?

Some days later, I had a visit – from Claire.

Exterior. ANNIE's house. Aggressive aeroplane noises from the flightpath. A woman knocks at the door. ANNIE opens.

ANNIE: Oh hi Claire, come in.

CLAIRE: No, I won't. I just wanted to talk to you about the book group if that's okay.

ANNIE: Yeh – I wanted to say thanks for having me the other day, it was so nice of you.

CLAIRE: Um, the book group is really important to us –

ANNIE: Sure.

CLAIRE: Because it's a place where we can get together, drink wine –

ANNIE: Mmm, and talk about books, yeh, I know, it's amazing.

CLAIRE: But also talk about other things.

ANNIE: Oh! Okay!

CLAIRE: The books are important / because it's a book group –

ANNIE: / obviously, because it's a book group. Claire I've got some ideas about things we could maybe read in the future, maybe *Infinite Jest* by David Foster Wallace...

CLAIRE: Never heard of him. But just – "hold that thought".

ANNIE: I'll email you.

CLAIRE: *(Grimaces.)* Because well, we would like the book group to be relaxing.

ANNIE: Relaxing.

CLAIRE: Yes and with you in it – well it's just not very relaxing.

ANNIE: –

CLAIRE: Because – you're a writer.

ANNIE: yeh

CLAIRE: And you really care about the books.

ANNIE: mhm

CLAIRE: And you have all these opinions about the books, and, well, it's quite intimidating.

ANNIE: What 'cause I've got opinions about books in a book group?

CLAIRE: Yeh – because you have ALL OF THESE OPINIONS – and I'm not stupid.

ANNIE: I know you're not.

CLAIRE: I've got a 2:1 in modern languages,

ANNIE: I know Claire, I know –

CLAIRE: and a masters, you don't have a masters do you.

ANNIE: No, I don't have a masters, no.

CLAIRE: Hmmm. But it's just like you're a professional jockey and you're trying to win the awards at a pony club do you understand?

ANNIE: No, I mean I've never ridden or anything so –

CLAIRE: I mean you just make us feel so stupid when we open our mouths!

ANNIE: No, that's not my intention.

CLAIRE: And we're not stupid!

ANNIE: I know, I'm sorry, that's not what I'm tryna do

CLAIRE: And THEN, when we talk about our husbands, or children, or houses, you just sit there with this supercilious look on your face

ANNIE: No I think that's just my face.

CLAIRE: Like you're being all superior.

ANNIE: No, that's not what I'm, that's not what's going on, look, if you – I know I can get a bit intense about the books if you need me to tone it down or anything.

CLAIRE: Well I'm just going to have to spell this out for you aren't I.

ANNIE: What?

CLAIRE: We have decided that we would be happier if you didn't come to the book group any more.

ANNIE: Okay.

CLAIRE: Listen, that's all I wanted to say, so –

ANNIE: Okay. Bye, bye Claire.

CLAIRE goes to leave then turns back.

CLAIRE: Actually, I don't suppose you're free to help out with the cake sale on Friday can you?

ANNIE: No!

CLAIRE: No. We didn't think you would be.

She goes.

ANNIE: Fucksake!

It became clear that I needed to add another item to my manifesto:

NICKI-AS-ANNIE:

4. KEEP YOUR INTEGRITY.

ANNIE: At this point I ran out of ideas for social integration. Also, I received this email from Verity.

VISUALS: SLIDE OF VERITY IN MOSCOW WITH TOM.

V/O:

Annie

I'm going to Moscow with Tom for 5 weeks.

Jonty will handle business in my absence. Have something excellent for me on my return please. I'm not going to continue this conversation indefinitely. FYI my top clients have three plays running concurrently all the time. That's what I would hope from you. Time to work Annie.

Verity. X O. X

ANNIE: So now I had to apply myself to writing not one but three West End Smashes simultaneously. And the rest of the time I helped my daughters develop their roots.

Trees montage. This film shows ANNIE's solitary daily life with her children, the Olive Trees. We see her negotiating massive rugby crowds carrying the trees, trying to get on a crowded train with the trees, giving her children a picnic, trampolining with them, giving them a bath, playing lego with them, reading to them. The whole sequence describes months and months of solitary parenting.

And this is the point at which the Walrus of Loneliness crashed unannounced into my life.

WALRUS and ANNIE on the bus. He is harassing her.
She tries to placate him with biscuits and drugs and booze.
He is aggressive. She is getting annoyed.

From the moment he barged through my front door, the
Walrus of Loneliness came everywhere with me. He was a
total pain in the arse – a constant, smelly, socially unskilled,
anarchic and laceratingly critical companion. Some kind of
yeti or bear, a Wild Thing but without the consolation of
having James Gandolfini inside him. He plagued me for 6
MONTHS, and got cockier every single day.

WALRUS in Richmond Park scene. ANNIE and WALRUS walk
in Richmond Park.

ANNIE: **So is this it then?**

WALRUS: **Yep.**

ANNIE: **How do I get rid of you?**

WALRUS: **It's quite difficult. Once I'm here, I tend to
settle.**

ANNIE: **Why now?**

WALRUS: **Your loneliness has become pathological
and self-perpetuating.**

ANNIE: **I'm not pathologically lonely. Watch this.**

A typically suburban woman, gilet, shirt, boots, colourful
chinos, approaches with a dog.

ANNIE: **That's a cool dog.**

The woman appears to just grimace at her in a hostile fashion.

ANNIE: **Right. I'm just going to sit here and try and
get on with some work.**

WALRUS: **I'll be right by your side.**

ANNIE: **Great (!)**

She sits to write.

Sometimes, however, haphazardly wonderful things happen.

JAY montage. A beautiful younger man, JAY, approaches ANNIE on the bench. Montage. They go for coffee, the WALRUS trying to sabotage their connection by swapping their coffees. They are getting on really well. They have a real connection. Later, they have sex outside in the trees. It's a reckless, zipless, pastoral outdoor fuck.

His name was Jay. He was a musician…just a couple of months – and 15 years – younger than me. He was passing through, sorting out some family stuff after a bereavement. He didn't know anyone in THOR. With Jay life felt abundant. I was mothering. I was creating. I was fucking refulgent. I was Best in Show.

SECOND JAY. JAY and ANNIE are at ANNIE's house. Playing charades with the Olive Trees. Montage. They are playing with the Olive Trees in the playground. JAY is helping ANNIE. They are happy. Later, JAY is reading to one of the Olive Trees before she goes to sleep. The WALRUS gets increasingly frustrated, and eventually leaves.

After a year or so I noticed that the Walrus wasn't bothering me any more. I don't know where he went.

WALRUS getting into a van, getting out and going to CLAIRE's house. Sign saying CLAIRE'S HOUSE.

THIRD JAY. ANNIE and JAY are happy in THOR. He piggy backs her across the road bridge as the sun sets. It's romantic, carefree. They are clearly crazy in love.

With Jay by my side as a co-conspirator, THOR seemed like an okay place. A place I could make my life tenable. A place I could live according to my manifesto.

I was working hard. I had my writing mojo back. I was hitting gold. I wrote a new play about love, with 23 fully developed characters. I sent an early draft to Verity. She didn't respond per se but I could feel in my heart that she was profoundly excited by my good news.

And about a year later, out of nowhere, Jay surprised me with THIS...

Chekhov bit. ANNIE and JAY are dressed in Chekhovian costumes, and the house has been changed to be like a Chekhov set – everything is draped in white.

JAY: I must go to New Cross.

ANNIE crumples.

I need to be part of an artistic community.
You know this. And. An opportunity has come up.
To do with my music.

Say something Anna Lisaveta.

ANNIE: If you go to New Cross, I will never see you again. No one from New Cross ever comes to Twickenham: Home of Rugby. You know this.

JAY: I don't want to leave you! Come with me! We could start a new life together in New Cross!

ANNIE: My life is here, in Twickenham: Home of Rugby.

JAY: Are you so determined to stay?

ANNIE: What time is your train?

JAY: It leaves in ten minutes.

ANNIE: Look at me. I want to etch your face into my soul so I never forget you. You have made my heart sing.

JAY: You have made me so very happy, Anna Lisaveta.

He goes to kiss her. She rebuffs him.

ANNIE: Goodbye, Dmitri Alexandreiovich.

JAY: I will always love you.

ANNIE: Wait!

She gets up and hands something to JAY.

It's poems. It's about us.

JAY: I will read it every day.

ANNIE: You will at first, and then you won't anymore.

JAY: Don't talk like that.

ANNIE: It's true.

JAY: I will write to you when I am settled in New Cross.

ANNIE: No.

JAY: No?

ANNIE: Write to the Olive Trees. You have meant so much to them.

They deserve a proper farewell.

JAY: I will write to them.

ANNIE: Thank you, Dmitri Alexandreiovich.

AUDIO: DOOR SLAM.

As soon as Jay shut the door, the Walrus was right back in my face, stenchier and more belligerent than ever.

WALRUS enters on stage. WALRUS DRONE.

As some of you will know, it's quite difficult to achieve your life goals when you're being constantly harassed by a flatulent, aggressive sea mammal. Representing for the girls became a challenge.

A melancholy film in which ANNIE is negotiating the girls, alone. As she puts them to bed, the WALRUS is aggressively playing the drums.

ANNIE: Why don't you help me?

WALRUS: That ain't my job.

ANNIE: And so did work because every time I opened my laptop to finish my excellent play about love I'd end up cranking, with the Walrus slow clapping me to climax.

Cranking video showing just this.

As if Jay had advertised a vacancy in my life, moths took over my house, and then mice did too. I couldn't believe that no one seemed to notice how badly I was doing, that I wasn't getting arrested, or visited by concerned women with clipboards.

One morning I got this email.

VISUALS: SHOT OF VERITY IN DUBAI.

Annie

I'm taking you off my books.

I wish you all the best in your future career. Jonty will handle all the rights issues for your existing plays, such as they are.

Verity. x o.

NICKI-AS-ANNIE: I need a new agent to help me sell my unfinished play.

I need money.

I need a sense of validation from my peers.

I need to be less morose for the Trees.

I need to achieve something creatively.

I need to achieve something creatively that can be made within my lifetime so that I can earn a commissioning fee of 7 whole thousand pounds so that my mortgage lender will get off my back and my bank manager will stop explaining to me that an overdraft limit is precisely that a limit that you can't go over and it doesn't matter if you are a person with fluid boundaries.

I need to stop the pain.

I need to kill the moths. I need to kill the mice.

I need to live according to my manifesto, in order to stop the pain.

I need to sleep.

ANNIE: After Jay left, I was a pure insomniac. It got so that I couldn't hear or see properly. I was underwater. My life was a dyspraxic subaqua ballet. I couldn't believe that the clipboard ladies still weren't coming, and that I was allowed to – no – expected to – take care of the Olive Trees all by myself.

I was entering a progressive degeneration phenomenon. A Downward Spiral.

One afternoon – one of many afternoons – spent not writing and instead weeping and doing "Which Kardashian are you?" quizzes online – I came across an article about reinventing yourself post-breakup. And so now, with the twistily convincing logic of the newly heartbroken, I figured that as I had managed to parent adequately, to write abundantly, and to live with integrity when Jay was around, what I quite clearly needed to do was to GET OUT THERE and find a replacement for him.

I signed up with some dating sites, a sense of tenuous optimism in my va-heart. In this great city of 9 million souls, surely Jay couldn't be the only person that I could connect with?

I spoke to this guy, Greg.

VISUALS: A SLIDE OF A GUY WITH A BIG CAR FROM TINDER.

And this guy, Andre.

A SLIDE OF ANOTHER GUY WITH A DOLPHIN FROM TINDER.

And this guy.

A SLIDE OF A STRANGELY SHAPED PENIS FROM TINDER.

I slept with this guy to shut him up about his tedious humanitarian projects.

A SLIDE OF A SMUG WHITE GUY HOLDING A CUTE BLACK BABY FROM TINDER.

I slept with this guy because – I can't remember why.

A SLIDE OF AN ABSOLUTELY GARGANTUAN PENIS FROM TINDER.

I didn't sleep with this guy because he was cagey about his job.

A SLIDE OF VLADIMIR PUTIN RIDING A DOLPHIN FROM TINDER.

There were more guys. Dating is expensive when you are paying childcare, and I was by this point massively in debt so I slept with as many of them as possible. You have to get Bang for your buck – right? Also during sex – even the most atrocious sex – the Walrus lost some of his potency. The problem was that as soon as the sex was done he came back even bigger and smellier than before.

One night, returning from a meeting with a theatre that had loved my last successful play but didn't want to commission my new one because the Walrus kept farting during the meeting so that the whole room stank of Loneliness, I picked up a charity mugger, and fellated him – efficiently – on the terrace of my local Pitcher and Piano.

Turns out that same P and P was now the HQ for the book group. ("Hi Claire!") And the book they were reading? David Foster Wallace's *Infinite Jest*.

As if I was being cosmically punished for my temporary and complete loss of any last shred of self-respect on

that evening, now one of the factors of the shitstorm decided to visit us again. One of Olive Trees has a chronic health condition – and sometimes it bites her hard for no discernible reason and everything must stop until she is better.

HOSPITAL FILM

ANNIE and the Olive Tree montage of hospital visits. She takes the Olive Tree, sometimes both Olive Trees, gets in and out of the van, goes in and out of the hospital. The hospital carpark machine says: HAVE A NICE DAY.

NICKI-as-ANNIE enters stage in her pyjamas, with Olive Tree. She sings the Billie Holiday Song 'Good Morning Heartache' and attends to the Olive Tree.

ANNIE enters as ANNIE but with the WALRUS head and hoodie.

As the WALRUS, ANNIE instructs the Tech Desk to play Lil Wayne's 'Gettin' Some Head' loudly over the top of the Billie Holiday, so it becomes increasingly difficult for NICKI-as-ANNIE to sing.

NICKI-AS-ANNIE: "Good morning heartache, you old gloomy sight…"

NICKI-AS-ANNIE continues to sing the song as it plays on the PA.

Then, NICKI-as-ANNIE turns to ANNIE-as-WALRUS.

Just leave me alone!

LONELINESS QUIZ. NICKI-as-ANNIE does a loneliness quiz online – we see this on the screen – and the result is that she gets the top score. CONGRATULATIONS! YOU HAVE EXTREME LONELINESS!

ANNIE takes off WALRUS head.

ANNIE: 6 months later, my daughter was better enough for me to go out on my birthday.

LONDON BRIDGE SCENE
ANNIE is getting ready to go out. She puts on makeup, a "sexy" dress, and febreezes herself.

BORDER PATROL ANT SCENE
ANNIE is at the border patrol between suburbia and London proper.

BORDER GUARD: **Passport please.**

ANNIE: **Yeah, sure. Here you go.**

BORDER GUARD: **Happy birthday to you.**

ANNIE: **Thank you! Have a lovely day! Bye!**

London train. ANNIE walks in London. She's really happy and excited.

The sun is shining and London has that sexy petrolly summer smell and shimmer and filth that makes me feel like the day is full of the potential for mischief. I have childcare till midnight. I am invincible.

I'm going to see a show with Lily – I'm really excited – I haven't seen her for a year because she's a 'nuclear, functionally grown up' friend – and then later I'm going to go on what is clearly a FIRST DATE. He's a guy called Elliot who I met at a workshop several years ago. We've been talking online. We share things. Taste. Humour. Some life experience. A similar age bracket. And because like me he works in THE ARTS it's clear that we are going to succeed in making this something. Something real and affective, not just obliterative fucking. I'm going to have the best birthday EVAH.

Lil texts me to say she can't meet – her childcare has fallen through. But I don't care.

NICKI-as-ANNIE – in the same sexy dress we see in the film – enters with a wildly oversized wine glass.

I order myself a small, 750ml glass of Malbec and settle down to watch the show which is funny and brutal and uncomfortably autobiographical.

I am determinedly having the BEST TIME.

I leave the theatre and walk into the bar and I see this.

JAY is there, with ELLE, his new girlfriend. They are doing a soundcheck. They kiss. ANNIE rushes out of the bar. JAY sees her and runs after her. She runs down the road and gives him the slip.

And I don't give any fucks. London is full of art and hedonism and possibility. Also, I'm meeting Elliot. We have an effortless connection, and the fact that he's already in a relationship seems like a surmountable obstacle at this point, and the fact that we haven't made exactly firm arrangements to meet seems like no thing, and the fact that I had not yet heard from him seems exciting and cazj and urban. I text him, concentrating really hard on spelling things properly and using correct grammar.

NICKI-AS-ANNIE: HI.

ELLIOT: *(Text.)* Hi

NICKI-AS-ANNIE: So. What's the sitch?

ELLIOT: *(Text.)* Happy Birthday Siddz

NICKI-AS-ANNIE: Thanks. What time we meeting.

ELLIOT: *(Text.)* Sorry

NICKI-AS-ANNIE: What

ELLIOT: *(Text.)* I can't meet you.

NICKI-AS-ANNIE: You know it's my birthday yeh

ELLIOT: *(Text.)* Yep I'm really sorry. You should totally just go out and get drunk and get laid. Rabbit emoticon, wine glass emoticon, smiley winky face emoticon.

WALRUS AND SEAL PUB SCENE
Same bit of film as at the top of the show. ANNIE sits in a pub getting absolutely hammered. Beside her is the WALRUS and his friend the Seal of Shame.

ANNIE: The thing about the Walrus of Loneliness is this. He can't lay you low all on his own. He can do his damnedest, but he can't quite change the waving to drowning, the ferocity of striving to the passivity of letting go. But the longer he's with you, the harder it is to resist the call of his boss, the sensuous and sadistic Seal of Shame. The Seal of Shame is the one that turns you from someone struggling into someone no longer struggling. The Seal of Shame has no mercy; she will annihilate you with her sweet nothings. The Seal of Shame saw an opportunity on that day, and she seized it: the shame of the fellatio, the shame of the random fucks of blindness, the shame of my fiscal failure and my professional paralysis, the shame of my daughter's illness, the shame of my failed marriage, the shame of ageing, the shame of being rejected, the shame of wanting, the shame of refusing to settle, the shame of fighting for a life that was not hemmed in by a picket fence of respectability and compromise, a life that burned bright. So, in the pub, on my own, the Walrus and the Seal sit with me, and they say this:

NICKI-AS-ANNIE: – look at you, Siddz, in your forties, thinking that people should give a fuck about your birthday when you don't even have anyone to spend your birthday with, look at you in that ridiculous outfit that was designed for like eighteen year olds, look at you shivering alone in this pub, really, is that what you think a good life is, a life of integrity?

NICKI-AS-ANNIE: (*Sending texts.*)

(*To LIL.*) Can't believe you bailed on me (SEND).

(*To VERITY.*) I'm so glad you don't represent me any more, you entitled public school duck. I am a fucking brilliant writer and if you can't recognise that you can stick your long thin cigarettes up your overprivileged anus and I hope you have a skiing accident falling off the top of Mont Blanc and end up a vegetable and your family wastes years with you on life support and one afternoon everyone thinks you've spoken but it's just your last stale breath coming out of your plummy cunty mouth XO XO X (SEND).

(To LIL.) and you didn't even call me
You are so cold cold cold colp cold cold frosty clog bitch
sometimes ain't ya
self absorbed bitch
it's my fucking birthday.

(To ELLIOT.) I hope your sham of a relationship dies a really slow, cancerous death that shatters your confidence and turns you in to a limpdick shadow of yourself haunted by failure. You're a coward and a liar. Fuck you, dickwad. (SEND).

(To LIL.) sorry but you should have called me
it's not cool
fucking ruinous!
sorry
hope the kids are okay (SEND).

SNORRICAM FILM
Rugby lads singing Queen, 'Bohemian Rhapsody' (badly). ANNIE, now dressed in the suburban woman's costume, makes her way back home. She is badly drunk. The SEAL and WALRUS accompany her, and watch her as she makes her way sobbing through the station, pisses in a bush, vomits in her bin. They then accompany her to her house. They do a dance. ANNIE decides to self harm. The WALRUS and the SEAL help her as she takes an overdose and prepares to cut her arm. Frank Sinatra's 'London by Night' plays.

NICKI-AS-ANNIE enters with phone as ANNIE on the film stumbles towards phone.

V/O: SAM ACCRINGTON M/F Friendly, polite, patient.

SAM ACCRINGTON: Hello is that Annie Simmons?

NICKI-AS-ANNIE: JAY is that you you cunt it's my birthday.
You know you never wrote to the Olive Trees.

SAM ACCRINGTON: Hello Miss Simmons this is Sam Accrington from HEL here.

NICKI-AS-ANNIE: So that's your new girlfriend? She looks about six by the dubs. Jay are you gonna sing happy birthday to me now? Happy Birthday to you Happy Birt...

SAM ACCRINGTON: Miss Simmons, this is Sam Accrington from HEL. Is this a bad time?

NICKI-AS-ANNIE: Jay what?

SAM ACCRINGTON: Miss Simmons, this is Sam Accrington. We just wanted to thank you for your generous support of HEL. Help End Loneliness.

NICKI-AS-ANNIE: Fuck I'm so sorry. I thought you were my ex boyfriend, who is a cunt. Please carry on.

SAM ACCRINGTON: Miss Simmons, a few months ago you gave a very generous donation to one of our street collectors.

NICKI-AS-ANNIE: What? Oh that. The question is who donated to whom?

SAM ACRRINGTON: What?

NICKI-AS-ANNIE: What? Doesn't matter. So now you want some more money right?

SAM ACCRINGTON: HAHA. Yes.

NICKI-AS-ANNIE: Okay Samaccrington do your spiel speak your spiiiell

SAM ACCRINGTON: We wanted to ask you if you would consider renewing your support and perhaps giving us a regular donation of ten pounds a month. Because Miss Simmons at the moment we are in a situation where we can only answer three out of four of calls made to us. Miss Simmons?

NICKI-AS-ANNIE: That's shit.

SAM ACCRINGTON: Yes. It is. And I don't know if you can imagine how that would feel if someone was so lonely that they couldn't bear it any more.

NICKI-AS-ANNIE: Well obviously I've never been in that kind of situation myself but I can imagine yeh it must be pretty grim.

SAM ACCRINGTON: And then not being able to get through to someone when they have been courageous enough to ask for help. Miss Simmons? Are you still there?

Miss Simmons? Are you still there?

NICKI-AS-ANNIE: Yes. I am still here. I am still here.

Shit. I need help

Dials 999.

VOICE: Emergency Services which service do you require?

NICKI-AS-ANNIE: Ambulance.

VOICE: Right so is the ambulance for yourself?

NICKI-AS-ANNIE: Yeh. I've been attacked by a Walrus and a Seal.

VOICE: Right. Are you safe?

NICKI-AS-ANNIE: They're still here. I'm scared.

VOICE: Where are you?

NICKI-AS-ANNIE: Twickenham: Home of Rugby.

NICKI-AS-ANNIE walks/staggers off.

ANNIE enters.

The winning takes time. The healing takes time. Loneliness is emotional drought and famine. It's a sign that you need to switch things up and nourish yourself with connection. If you ignore it, it can slowly kill you. Loneliness is not the same as depression but they are common bedfellows. The chronically lonely brain is hyper alert for social threat: you feel attacked and vilified, making you blind to the kindness that surrounds you. The chronically lonely brain turns you into a paranoid, hostile recluse. Paranoid hostile recluses are arguably NOT the most joyous company, so loneliness breeds loneliness. An intervention is necessary. An awareness. A naming of parts.

My loneliness is a Walrus. It comes and it goes still, but I know it now. It guzzles on clams of perfectionism, worms of maternal sacrifice, sea cucumbers of financial insecurity, cephalopods of zone 5 isolation, polar cod of suburban nuclearity, and benthic invertebrates of pride. I fed my Walrus generously and inadvertently, until he grew so corpulent the Seal of Shame had to dive in and finish me, so in order to slim him down, gradually, safely, I've had to look at all these things. The manifesto has had to be amended. The grandiosity of my solo attempts to excel at mothering, at art, at love, have had to be challenged in order for me to escape the suburbs of my own existence.

NICKI-AS-ANNIE comes on cleaned up, sober, and in new clothes.

NICKI-AS-ANNIE: Idea for a new show. Idea for a new autobiographical show. Idea for a new autobiographical show performed by me.

Hello my name is Annie Siddons. A few years ago I had a visitor.

ANNIE: As part of this process I've trained as a volunteer with a charity that for the purpose of this show I will call HELP END LONELINESS. We're trained not to fix, not to advise, not to offer mindfulness colouring books, just to listen, to hear people's stories, to offer an auditory hug.

So. This is the new Annifesto:

1. Be a good enough mother.
2. Make good art. Collaborate.
3. Love and connect, in as many different ways as you can.
4. Keep your integrity.

Thank you so much for coming.

ENDS.

Printed in the USA
CPSIA information can be obtained
at www.ICGtesting.com
LVHW020943171024
794056LV00003B/940